GREAT DEBATES
TOUGH QUESTIONS / SMART HISTORY

OUR
MILITARY

By
Geoffrey C. Harrison
and
Thomas F. Scott

NORWOODHOUSE PRESS

CHICAGO, ILLINOIS

Norwood House Press
PO Box 316598
Chicago, Illinois 60631

For information regarding Norwood House Press, please visit our website at:
www.norwoodhousepress.com or call 866-565-2900.

Photo credits:
Library of Congress (4, 10, 12, 13, 16, 17, 18, 21, 22, 23, 24, 29, 34, 35, 36, 37, 43 both, 44);
Dwight D. Eisenhower Presidential Library & Museum (28); Ronald Reagan Presidential Library
(29); Associated Press (38, 40, 41).

Cover Photos: Mark Ralston/AFP/Getty Images (left), Simon Lim/AFP/Getty Images (right).

Edited by Mark Stewart and Mike Kennedy.
Designed by Ron Jaffe.
Special thanks to Content Consultant Kim Greene.

Library of Congress Cataloging-in-Publication Data

Harrison, Geoffrey.
  Our military / by Geoffrey Harrison and Thomas F. Scott; edited by Mark
Stewart and Mike Kennedy.
     pages cm. -- (Great debates)
  Includes bibliographical references and index.
  Summary: "Informational text uses a historical framework to discuss
issues surrounding the role of the United States military. Sections include
opinions from notable Americans on various sides of the issue followed by
encouragement for readers to analyze each opinion."— Provided by the
publisher.
  ISBN 978-1-59953-590-6 (library edition : alk. paper) --
  ISBN 978-1-60357-570-6 (ebook)
1. United States--Armed Forces--Juvenile literature. 2. National security--
United States--Juvenile literature. 3. United States--Military policy--Juvenile
literature. I. Scott, Thomas F. II. Stewart, Mark, 1960- III. Kennedy, Mike,
1965- IV. Title.
  UA23.H3647 2013
  355.00973--dc23
                                        2013016656

COVER: Some believe that the role of the U.S. military is to provide
security for the country. Others think we should use the military to
expand our reach around the world.

Contents

INTRODUCTION

Note: Words that are **bolded** in the text are defined in the glossary.

INTRODUCTION

We have issues ...

History doesn't just happen. It isn't made simply with the delivery of a speech or the stroke of a pen. If you look closely at every important event in the story of America, you are likely to discover deep thinking, courageous action, powerful emotion ... and great debates.

This book explores the ongoing debate about the role of the United States military. This issue has touched almost every American in a very personal way for more than two centuries. When U.S. soldiers pick up a weapon in the nation's defense, they make a commitment to fight (and maybe die) as a matter of duty and honor. Sometimes our military fights because we are attacked, and sometimes our military takes the fight to our enemies before they have the chance to attack us. Either way, ideas on what's worth fighting for and how to fight can differ dramatically. Some of the arguments you read about in this book will be familiar—people have been making them for more than a century. Other issues are more recent.

This illustration shows George Washington (left) on horseback in Valley Forge, Pennsylvania. Washington was America's first military hero.

Join the Debate

Debate is the art of discussing a controversial topic using logic and reason. One side takes the affirmative side of an issue and the other takes the negative side. Remember, however, that a great debate does not necessarily need to be an argument—often it is a matter of opinion, with each side supporting its viewpoint with facts. The key is to gather enough information to create a strong opinion. Out in the real world, debate has fewer rules and can get noisy and ugly. But on the big issues in America, debate is often how compromises are made and things get done.

America's military history began at a time when the region was still an English colony. During the 1600s and early 1700s, colonists were sometimes asked to form **militias** and fight for England. Often these battles were against Native Americans, who were being pushed off their tribal lands by European settlers. In 1754, war broke out between England and France (and its ally, Spain). In America, it was known as the **French and Indian War**, which lasted nine years.

After the French and Indian War, American colonists believed they had earned the full rights of British citizenship. When these rights were denied, they fought and won their freedom from England. From 1775 to 1783, George Washington led an army of untrained farmers and defeated the greatest military power in the world. It was the willingness of the American soldiers to sacrifice for their

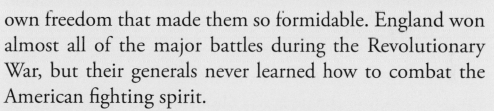

Make Your Case

In Chapter 2 through Chapter 5, you will find special sections entitled **Make Your Case**. Each one highlights different sides of the debate on our military, using quotes from prominent Americans. **Make Your Case** lets you analyze the speaker's point of view … and challenges you to form an opinion of your own. You'll find additional famous opinion-makers on the military debate in Chapter 7.

own freedom that made them so formidable. England won almost all of the major battles during the Revolutionary War, but their generals never learned how to combat the American fighting spirit.

At the end of the war, a debate began about the size, strength, and purpose of the military. A "standing" army is very expensive to maintain. Soldiers have to be housed, fed, clothed, trained, and supplied with the weapons they need to do their jobs. The American people pay the bill through their tax dollars. That means they have a say in how the military looks and operates. No one argues about the importance of an army for defending the country from attack. But when else should America's military be used? Keep this in mind as you read about these great debates.

1

Should our military focus on defense or conquest?

In the late 1700s and early 1800s, England, France, and Spain all cast hungry eyes on the natural resources of North America. That made the role of the U.S. military simple: defend the nation from its enemies. The United States fended off these foreign powers and started to expand west to the Pacific Ocean. When America met resistance, the military was called in. When a new generation of leaders emerged, the focus of the armed forces shifted to meet their needs, including the push to colonize to the West. This led to the first great debate on the role of our military …

AFFIRMATIVE SIDE

Defense of the nation is the role of our military. However, if the goal of the nation is to grow in size and power, then we must build an army and navy to protect our economic interests. If another country tries to stop America with military force, then our military must be trained and ready to defeat that enemy.

Enemies All Around

The U.S. felt anything but secure in the years after the Revolutionary War. The English controlled the Atlantic Ocean with their navy and stationed soldiers in Canada and the Caribbean Islands. Meanwhile, the people of France united to overthrow their king, and from the chaos came a dangerous military leader, Napoleon Bonaparte. He hoped to conquer Europe, and also had plans to extend the French Empire to the southern and central parts of America.

The U.S. dealt with these threats in different ways. In 1803, America bought French territory that covered all or part of 15 current states. The Louisiana Purchase cost $15 million, or about 3 cents an acre. This addition of territory did not require our military to fire a single shot. Most of the "battles" took place in Washington, D.C., where many politicians opposed the deal. They believed that the Constitution did not give America the right to spend the people's money that way.

NEGATIVE SIDE

We are not conquerors. We gained our freedom from a nation that survived by conquering other people. If we wish to expand our influence over North America, let it be done through friendly negotiation, treaties, and the promise of freedom—not at the end of a bayonet.

The *U.S.S. Constitution* takes control of a British ship and pulls it back to port during the War of 1812.

Dealing with the English was more complicated. They were threatened by the Louisiana Purchase and feared America might try to take Canada from them. Indeed, **expansionists** in the U.S. government did look eagerly to the north. The English responded by attacking American shipping lanes and forcing sailors into service in England's war against Napoleon and the French. England also encouraged Native American tribes to attack American settlers along the frontier. The U.S. reacted by declaring war. The **War of 1812** lasted until 1814 and ended in a **stalemate**; both sides agreed to end the hostilities and eventually became important allies.

Manifest Destiny

After standing firm against England, Americans gained a new sense of national pride and security. Some now

Make Your Case

"We must march from Texas straight to the Pacific Ocean, and be bounded only by its roaring wave ... It is the destiny of the white race."

▶ *William Giles, 1847*

Giles was a Senator from Virginia. He agreed with many in the U.S. who thought that **Manifest Destiny** was the best military strategy for the country.

Was Manifest Destiny a valid reason for the U.S. to expand its territory?

believed the North American continent was theirs for the taking. This idea, known as Manifest Destiny, meant that America was destined to rule from the Atlantic to the Pacific.

Manifest Destiny played a role in how the U.S. dealt with Spain, which had spent decades colonizing parts of North America, Central America, and South America. The Spanish empire, however, was in decline. In the early 1800s, Spain handed over the parts of Florida and Louisiana it still controlled. From 1810 to 1830, Spain lost all of its holdings in South America and Central America to independence movements, including one in Mexico. At the time, Mexico stretched from current-day Texas north and west all the way to the Canadian border, including everything west of the Rocky Mountains. The U.S. saw an opportunity to expand its territory and increase its power.

Make Your Case

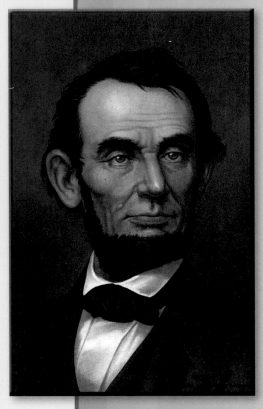

"Allow a president to invade a neighboring nation whenever he shall deem it necessary to repel an invasion ... and you allow him to make war at pleasure."

► *Abraham Lincoln, 1848*

The 1846 conflict with Mexico marked the first time that a large group of Americans opposed a war for moral reasons. Lincoln, at the time an Illinois Congressman, feared the war's grave consequences. He felt that President James Polk had overstepped his power, and knew that the vast territory America took from Mexico would trigger an argument about the future of slavery.

Should the decision to go to war be a political one or a military one?

Not everyone believed in Manifest Destiny. The Whig party (a forerunner of today's Republican party) opposed this idea. Whigs felt that America should build up its industrial might before it expanded. Growing too fast, they feared, might actually weaken the nation. Democrats disagreed, claiming that the resources won with new territory were the best way to strengthen the country. Acting on orders from President Polk, General Zachary Taylor provoked the Mexican army into an attack near the Texas border. The U.S. declared war on Mexico in 1846, and claimed victory two years later. In turn, the nation secured territories that are today known as California, New Mexico, Arizona, Nevada, Utah, and parts of Wyoming and Colorado.

Now consider *this* ...

The idea of using the military to conquer new lands did not sit well with all Americans. In fact, to many, Manifest Destiny seemed un-American. For example, the writer Henry David Thoreau (right) refused to pay his taxes because he did not want to fund the war with Mexico. Thoreau and others believed the purpose of the war was to spread the inhuman practice of slavery from the Atlantic to the Pacific. Thoreau, who was jailed for his actions, wrote an essay about his experience called *Civil Disobedience.*

As a "celebrity" in his time, Thoreau decided that going to jail was the best way to make his point. **What forms of anti-war protest are most effective for non-celebrities?**

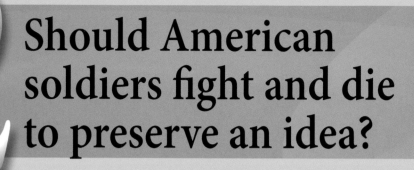

2 Should American soldiers fight and die to preserve an idea?

As the country expanded westward, Southern leaders wanted the new states to determine their own destiny and adopt slavery. Meanwhile, a movement to abolish slavery gained strength in the North. In 1860, Abraham Lincoln won the presidential election. Afraid that Lincoln would abolish slavery, the South broke away from the United States and formed the Confederate States of America. Soon after, Confederate forces attacked a Union fort in South Carolina. As the North prepared for war, people began a new debate about the military …

AFFIRMATIVE SIDE

The country began with a fight for freedom, so there is nothing wrong with asking American soldiers to fight and die for a cause. Keeping the states "united" is crucial. If the South is allowed to set up its own country, a battle for control of the Mississippi River and all the land to the west will ensue. Better to settle both issues now.

An Isolated South

The Civil War lasted from 1861 to 1865 and took more than 700,000 lives. The cotton-growing states of the South had built their economies on slave labor. They feared that an end to slavery would weaken them, and that the North would gain economic power. The leaders of the Confederacy believed that the nations of Europe would come to their aid. Many countries on the other side of the Atlantic depended on cotton from the South for their factories. However, when war broke out, the South found it had no allies overseas. The people of European nations despised the idea of slavery. There was little chance they would take up arms in defense of the South.

The goal of the Union Army in the Civil War was to defeat the Confederate States Army. How this was accomplished raised important questions about the role of the military. General William Sherman led Union forces on a path of destruction through the Southeast.

NEGATIVE SIDE

You can ask people to fight and die for a cause, but can you force them to? By drafting soldiers to fight against slavery, the Union Army has decided to trade the lives of one group of people for the lives of another. That violates the freedom we enjoy as Americans.

African-American soldiers were an important part of the
Union Army during the Civil War.

His soldiers burned and looted entire towns, and destroyed the **infrastructure** of the region. Sherman not only defeated the South's armies, he brought death and suffering to its people.

The End of Slavery

In 1863, President Lincoln issued the Emancipation Proclamation, which freed the slaves in the U.S. Lincoln was concerned that this might be viewed as a wartime measure, so he pushed for a new **amendment** to the Constitution banning slavery everywhere, once and for all. In 1865, with the war drawing to a close, Congress passed the 13th Amendment. It said that slavery could no longer exist in America or in any other place it controlled.

After the war, the Southern states were invited back into the Union. Although slavery had been abolished, many of these states passed laws that denied former slaves the basic rights of American citizens. Before long, Congress passed the 14th Amendment. It spelled out the rights of African Americans, including the rights to vote and to own land. To protect these rights, the Union Army was sent into the South, and 10 states were placed under military control.

Make Your Case

"[I] am quite certain that the crimes of this guilty land will never be purged away but with blood."

► *John Brown, 1859*

Brown was a Southerner who wanted to end slavery, which helped make him a controversial figure in the **abolitionist movement**. Most believed it could be done peacefully. Brown thought it would take a war and did his best to start one. This quote was among his final words before he was hanged for treason. Hangings were a common form of punishment in the South.

Should Brown's attempts to spark a violent revolt over slavery have been punished by death?

Make Your Case

Sam'l S. Cox

Ohio.

204

"This government is a government of white men ... The men who made it never intended by anything they did, to place the black race on an equality with the white."

► *Samuel Cox, 1862*

Cox was an Ohio Congressman who belonged to the Copperheads, a group of northern politicians that opposed the Civil War. They did not believe the fight over slavery was worth the cost in money and lives lost. They also felt using our military on American soil went against the Constitution. Several Copperheads were arrested for spreading their views.

Is opposition to armed conflict healthy—and/or necessary—in a democracy?

Union troops remained in the South until 1877. They were treated as unwelcomed guests, and were the targets of violence by groups of former Confederate soldiers. When these groups attacked African Americans—and also politicians who supported the changes taking place in the South—there was little that could be done to protect them. Another challenge faced by our military during this era was lawsuits brought by Southern citizens against Union soldiers when they tried to enforce the new laws. Judges and lawyers still hostile to the North allowed these suits to be heard. The court cases were expensive and brought up complicated legal questions. In many instances, Union soldiers chose not to enforce the law for fear that they would be sued.

Now consider *this* ...

The years that followed the Civil War were known as the Reconstruction Era. During this time, the military ran elections and oversaw local governments in the former slave states. Union soldiers also tried to protect African Americans from violence. The soldiers were part of a 20,000-person "police" force. Using the military to enforce laws within the U.S. was very controversial in the North and the South. *What might the reaction be in your town if the military took over to make sure local laws were enforced?*

Is the freedom of others worth fighting for?

In the 30 years following the Civil War, America focused on rebuilding its economy, healing its wounds, and becoming a world power. This changed the role of the military. In 1898, the nation went to war with Spain to defend the people of Cuba, who were trying to win their independence from their Spanish conquerors. U.S. forces defeated Spain and sent an important signal to the world: America would take up arms to protect the freedom of people in foreign lands. It also started a debate that would define the country's role throughout the 20th century …

AFFIRMATIVE SIDE

America stands for freedom. How can we just watch while others are being robbed of theirs? The U.S. is separated from other world powers by two oceans. It is blessed with friendly neighbors. The reason for building a strong military is to defend our principles.

President Woodrow Wilson asks Congress to declare war on Germany. Wilson did not want to enter World War I, but by 1917 he had little choice.

World War I

In 1914, World War I exploded in Europe, with England and France joining forces against Germany. At first, President Woodrow Wilson tried to keep America out of the fighting. Most Americans agreed, arguing the war was not worth American lives. Those who believed the U.S. should get involved used **propaganda** to make German soldiers look like monsters. After entering the neutral country of Belgium, they committed many **atrocities** against the Belgians. Homes were destroyed, civilians were executed, women and children were treated with terrible cruelty, and one of Europe's great medieval libraries was set ablaze.

NEGATIVE SIDE

If other countries choose to attack their neighbors or victimize their own people, why should the U.S. get involved? We are not the world's police force. The more people living under harsh rule, the more America will shine as an example of freedom. Our military should not be used to solve someone else's problems.

"We believe in an independent destiny for America ... American boys will not be sent across the ocean to die so that England or Germany or France or Spain may dominate the other nations."

▶ *Charles Lindbergh, 1941*

The horrors of World War I gave rise to a strong **isolationist** movement in the United States. Charles Lindbergh, a famous American aviator, was one of the people who thought America should stay out of the squabbles of other countries. He did not think our military should get involved in World War II.

What are the advantages of an isolationist policy?

Incidents of German war crimes convinced President Wilson to join England, France, and their allies against Germany. So too did the idea that Germany and its allies were dictators fighting against free and democratic people. American forces entered the war in 1917. By that time, it had become a stalemate. Within 18 months, the balance on the battlefield had tipped. Fearing an invasion of its homeland, Germany agreed to end the war in the fall of 1918.

World War II

Two decades later, the world stood on the brink of war once again. This time, it was President Franklin Roosevelt who faced a difficult decision about what America should do. Japan invaded China and started to build a Pacific empire. More than 200,000 Chinese were killed during the invasion. In Europe, Germany assembled a powerful army and air force under dictator Adolf Hitler. His plan called for

Make Your Case

"It becomes clearer and clearer that the world will be a shabby and dangerous place to live in—yes, even for Americans to live in—if it is ruled by force in the hands of a few … I hope that we shall have fewer American ostriches in our midst. It is not good for the ultimate health of ostriches to bury their heads in the sand."

▶ *Franklin Roosevelt, 1910*

President Roosevelt believed that ignoring the war in Europe was a mistake. Waiting to get our military involved, he argued, would only make things worse for America in the future.

Should we enter a war as soon as innocent lives are at stake, or should we wait until our national interests are threatened?

The attack on Pearl Harbor shocked the nation and
drew the U.S. into World War II.

the Germans to "purify" Europe of Jewish people, Gypsies,
and the Slavic people of Eastern Europe. When the German
army invaded a country, these people were deprived of their
freedom—and often killed or enslaved.

Hitler rose to power during the years of the **Great
Depression**, when the American economy was in crisis.
Congress passed four **neutrality acts** from 1935 to 1939,
hoping to make it impossible for the U.S. military to get
drawn into war. President Roosevelt disagreed. When World
War II began in 1939, he wanted to stop the Germans and
Japanese, but he didn't have enough support. The war raged
for two years before Japan attacked the U.S. naval base at

Pearl Harbor in Hawaii on December 7, 1941. That ended the debate—America was going to war.

Within two years, the U.S. and its allies gained the upper hand. In 1945, Germany and Japan surrendered. The cost of World War II in human lives was staggering. Around 60 million people were killed; fewer than half were soldiers. Many in the military believed that America had waited too long to enter the war. They were unwilling to make this mistake again. This commitment to protect those who can't defend themselves did not go unnoticed. In fact, the threat of American intervention convinced many countries to solve their differences without going to war.

Now consider *this* ...

In the final months of World War II, American soldiers found several death camps run by the Germans. An estimated 6 million Jewish people were killed in what has come to be known as the Holocaust. Another 6 million people (and possibly many more) were killed or starved to death because of their ethnicity or religion. Today, this is known as "ethnic cleansing"—an attempt to erase all evidence of a minority and its culture from a country. It has often been called a crime against humanity. **Does the military have a duty to protect victims of ethnic cleansing, even if it takes military action against another government?**

4 Is the business of war good for our country?

T he lessons learned from World War II guaranteed that the United States would continue increasing the size and strength of its military. A well-prepared, well-equipped military was important for the country's defense. It also pumped billions of dollars into the American economy. Some believe that the build-up for World War II rescued the U.S. from the grip of the Great Depression. Starting in the late-1940s—and continuing to today—America's military and industrial leaders have enjoyed a very close partnership. This has raised many important questions in the debate …

AFFIRMATIVE SIDE

America's power comes from the strength of its economy, so our military should help make the economy strong. Manufacturing weapons and equipment creates jobs. It also encourages companies to create new products for our armed forces (and also for the armed forces of our allies).

The Military-Industrial Complex

One of the heroes of World War II was General Dwight Eisenhower. He was elected president in 1952 and served for two terms during the early years of the Cold War, a four-decade period when the U.S and Soviet Union—a group of countries controlled by present-day Russia—competed for power around the world. The two powers didn't fight each other directly, but each spent billions building up its weapons technology and military might. America prospered during Eisenhower's years in office, partly because of the jobs created by the military.

In Eisenhower's farewell speech, he warned America about the dangers of the Military-Industrial Complex. He believed there was a "triangle" of power in the U.S. formed by the military, the arms industry, and politicians. The military relied on politicians to boost its budget. The arms industry depended on military budgets to make big profits.

NEGATIVE SIDE

How many ships, planes, and nuclear weapons do we really need? Companies keep making products for the military, and the military keeps buying them, even when there is no war to fight. That is a waste of American tax dollars.

Make Your Case

"Every gun that is made, every warship launched, every rocket fired signifies in the final sense, a theft from those who hunger and are not fed, those who are cold and are not clothed."

▶ *Dwight Eisenhower, 1953*

President Eisenhower warned against out-of-control military spending. He believed that an equal balance between the military and the American economy was the best defense in the Cold War.

Is having a powerful military more important than having a strong economy?

Politicians relied on donations of money to pay for re-election campaigns—much of which came from companies in the military industry. Eisenhower feared this triangular relationship would lead to waste, corruption, higher taxes, and less money for important social programs at home in America.

The A-1 tank, which became one of the nation's most effective weapons, is an example of the military spending its money wisely.

High Points & Low Points

Naturally, the military wants the most advanced weapons available. Companies compete to make those products, hoping to win a valuable contract from the government. This has produced amazing results, including the F-15 fighter jet, the B-2 stealth bomber, the Apache attack helicopter, and the

Make Your Case

"It's far better to prevent a crisis than to have to face it unprepared at the last moment. That's why we have an overriding moral obligation to invest now … in restoring America's strength to keep the peace and preserve our freedom."

▶ *Ronald Reagan, 1983*

Like Eisenhower, President Reagan held office during the Cold War with the Soviet Union. But during the 1980s, Reagan looked at the country's poor economy and under-equipped military, and said that more defense spending would solve both problems.

Is it right to increase the military's budget to help the economy—and what are the risks in doing so?

A-1 tank. The cost of developing these weapons can be very high, but as long as the results are good, many goals are met. The military gets what it needs, jobs are created and that money helps keep the economy healthy.

The problem comes when weapons and technology don't produce the desired results. Sometimes, a good idea never quite makes it from the drawing board to the battlefield. Rather than cancelling these projects, however, politicians often agree to keep spending more money to "fix" the problem. In the worst cases, projects with no military value end up costing hundreds of millions of dollars before they are finally cancelled. Some have cost more than $1 billion.

Now consider *this* …

The U.S. military's most advanced weapons are "smart weapons"—the kinds that use lasers to find their targets. These weapons are very expensive to build. For example, the U.S. Navy pays more than $1 million for each Tomahawk **cruise missile** it launches. Of course, every dollar spent on a cruise missile is a dollar that could also go to something that benefits Americans in some other way, such as education or road-building. Part of the value of smart weapons is that they save lives by keeping soldiers out of harm's way. *But at what point does a smart weapon become too expensive?*

Should our military send troops overseas in the name of national security?

Our military learned many lessons during World War II. Among the most important was that waiting to fight a war can give an enemy the chance to build up great strength. At the end of World War II, Germany was very close to making powerful weapons that could have been used against American cities. Had the United States entered the war later than it did, those weapons might have been perfected. Since then, the U.S. military has fought wars in faraway places, all in the name of national security. Whenever these conflicts occur, they trigger a great debate …

AFFIRMATIVE SIDE

Meeting an enemy overseas is a far better option than waiting until that enemy reaches American soil. Part of being a powerful country is keeping small problems from becoming big threats. When political and economic measures fail, it is the duty of our military to do its job.

The Cold War

The Cold War between the Americans and Soviets came down to two ideas: **Capitalism** vs. **Communism**. In the decades following World War II, America was the leading capitalist power. The Soviet Union was the leading Communist power (along with the People's Republic of China). During the Cold War, the U.S. and Soviet Union avoided direct conflict. Each side had built up large arsenals of nuclear weapons. Using these weapons would have caused incredible destruction and loss of life. In other words, there could be no "winners" when the dust settled. This changed the role of the military. Wherever Communism threatened democratic governments in foreign lands, America sent soldiers, weapons, equipment, and money.

In 1950, North Korea—a Communist neighbor of the Soviet Union—launched an attack on South Korea. The U.S. committed more than 300,000 soldiers to the region.

NEGATIVE SIDE

Who decides what is a threat to American soil and what is not? We should find ways to control our enemies without putting lives on the line. It's unfair to ask young men and women to risk their lives when national security isn't truly at risk.

Americans often took to the streets to protest the Vietnam War.

The Korean War lasted three years. More than 30,000 Americans died in battle. In 1961, North Vietnam began sending large numbers of Communist forces into South Vietnam. The U.S. helped the South Vietnamese, first with advisors and later with troops. The Vietnam War lasted more than a decade, and cost nearly 60,000 American lives. Many people changed their view of the military during this era. They felt they were misled about the Vietnam War. Some still distrust the military to this day.

Projecting Power

Starting in the 1980s, conflicts in the Middle East created a different kind of threat to national security. The U.S. economy was powered by oil, and this region was a key inexpensive resource. At first, the military was sent overseas to keep the peace. But American soldiers were often viewed in the **Muslim** world as invaders. U.S. support of the Jewish state of Israel only made matters worse.

Many memorials were created after the 9–11 attacks, including this one at the plane crash site in Pennsylvania.

The role of the U.S. military in the Middle East continued to grow, change, and become even more complicated. In 1990, Iraq invaded the neighboring country of Kuwait, which was an important oil-producing ally of the U.S. In 1991, America led a coalition of forces into battle to free Kuwait, and destroy the Iraqi military.

The Gulf War was hailed as a great victory, but it had grave consequences. The presence of American forces in Saudi Arabia enraged **religious extremists**. One group, calling itself Al Qaeda (in Arabic, *The Base*), hoped to gain influence in the Muslim world by waging war against the U.S. Al Qaeda launched several terrorist attacks, including two against the World Trade Center in New York City. The second, on September 11, 2001, killed more than 3,000 Americans. On that same day, a hijacked plane slammed into the Pentagon in Washington, D.C., and another was headed toward the U.S. Capitol before passengers forced it to crash in Pennsylvania.

The terror attacks of 9–11 shook the nation. To many, they showed the importance of meeting threats overseas before they reached American soil. Our military began fighting in Afghanistan, where the **Taliban** government had allowed Al Qaeda to train terrorists and plan attacks.

Make Your Case

"America must not ignore the threat gathering against us. Facing clear evidence of peril, we cannot wait for the final proof, the smoking gun that could come in the form of a mushroom cloud."

▶ *George W. Bush, 2002*

President Bush sent troops into Iraq in 2003 in the name of national security. He believed that Iraqi dictator Saddam Hussein had weapons of mass destruction and planned to use them against the U.S. or sell them to terrorists.

Even though there were no weapons of mass destruction, was the U.S. right to attack Iraq?

In 2003, the U.S. invaded Iraq. Some believed that Iraqi president Saddam Hussein was creating nuclear and chemical weapons that would be used against Americans. (Afterwards, it was learned that no such weapons existed.) In Afghanistan and Iraq, the military found itself playing a new role. Instead of fighting, winning, and coming home, the troops stayed in foreign countries in huge numbers. Their job was to hunt down terrorists and keep these areas from falling into the hands of hostile forces.

Make Your Case

"I oppose the Iraq war, just as I opposed the Vietnam War, because these two conflicts have weakened the U.S. and diminished our standing in the world and our national security."

▶ *George McGovern, 2007*

McGovern was a U.S. Senator from North Dakota during the Vietnam War. He also fought in World War II. McGovern believed the Iraq War was a poor use of our military.

Is it wise to keep our troops in foreign countries once our military goals have been achieved?

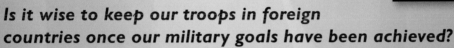

Now consider *this* ...

In earlier wars, young people were drafted to build up the U.S. military. But the armed forces in Iraq and Afghanistan were made up entirely of volunteers. It turned out that there simply were not enough soldiers to keep the peace in these countries, so the U.S. had to hire private companies to pick up the slack. This sent the military budget soaring. America borrowed trillions of dollars to pay this growing bill. In years past, military action had helped the economy. Now it was having a damaging effect. *If we do not have enough soldiers to guarantee national security, is restarting the draft a good option?*

6 Find your voice

In recent years, three issues have been at the center of the debate surrounding the U.S. military. These are complicated questions that invite many points of view. Much like the military debates over the last 200 years, they involve economics, politics, powerful fears, and strong emotions. There is a very good chance that people will be debating these issues throughout your lifetime.

Some Americans believe that war should never be looked at as a solution to the world's problems.

Are we fighting for corporations?

Critics of America's involvement in the Middle East often wonder why the U.S. is "really" there. Our military's job is to keep Americans safe from terrorist threats at home and overseas. But part of national security also involves making sure that oil keeps flowing from this region. If it doesn't, the cost of oil from other sources would rise sharply and damage the U.S. economy. Is this a cause worth dying for? Some point out that the U.S. is also fighting for the rights of millions of people who enjoy very little freedom. Others believe that the billions spent in the Middle East can be used to develop different types of energy closer to home.

When is torture okay?

The United Nations considers torture of prisoners a war crime. Around the world, about 60 percent of people believe that torture is wrong in any circumstance. Those who say prisoners can be subjected to "enhanced **interrogation**" mostly focus on captured terrorists who may have information that could stop an attack on civilians. Even then, there is strong disagreement on what constitutes torture. In 2004, the U.S. Assistant Attorney General approved several interrogation techniques against terrorists. When President

Barack Obama took office in 2009, he forbid the military from using techniques such as **waterboarding**.

What should America's policy for the use of drones be?

A drone is an unmanned aircraft used by the military to watch the movements of enemies on the ground. Drones can stay aloft for many hours without using much fuel. They are often controlled by "pilots" thousands of miles away. Some drones are armed with missiles.

Throughout the War on Terror (launched after the attacks on September 11, 2001), the U.S. military has used drones to attack and kill terrorists, including two in Yemen who also happened to be American citizens. This makes many wonder whether the military should be limited when it comes to the use of drones. Drones are already used in the U.S. to watch borders, and help fight forest fires. Most Americans approve of these uses. But would they approve of using drones to attack Americans on American soil?

A military commander receives training for operating a drone.

The debate about the U.S. military has divided Americans for centuries. People on both sides are passionate about their views.

All the issues in this chapter are being discussed right now as part of the debate on the role of the U.S. military. Can America continue to afford to send troops into unstable areas in the name of national security? Who is the enemy and how should they be treated? When soldiers are replaced with "smart" machines, does that change how our leaders decide when to go to war? Now is the time to join the national conversation. Think about these issues and consider both sides of these debates. Where do you stand? One day soon— through the candidates you support, the dollars you spend, and your own personal feelings about the military— you will have a voice!

7 Point — Counterpoint

America's policy on the military has been greatly influenced by public opinion over the years. That opinion is shaped by many factors, including personal experience, common sense, and what others write or have to say. We think about the different sides of an issue. We look at how it affects us, our family members, and our friends. We consider the best solutions. And we weigh what the smartest and most influential people believe.

This was true in the 1700s and 1800s, when Americans got their information from pamphlets, newspapers, and speeches. It was true in the 1900s, when radio and television brought ideas to an even wider audience. It remains true today, as we scan websites, blogs, and social media. The voices in this chapter have helped shape the debate on the military. The words may be a little different, but the passion behind them would fit in any era ...

"We are called upon by every consideration of duty and patriotism to **vindicate** with decision the honor, the rights, and the interests of our country."
James Polk (left), 1846

"It is harder to preserve than to obtain liberty."
John Calhoun (right), 1846

President Polk used a skirmish near the Texas border as an excuse to launch an all-out invasion of Mexico in 1846. While he claimed the U.S. military was marching into another country to uphold the ideas of honor and duty, the invasion was really about winning the territory it coveted. Calhoun was an important political leader in the early 1800s. He believed that the military should only be used to preserve our freedom. While Calhoun supported the War of 1812, he opposed the Mexican War in 1846.

What should be the focus of the military: defending the nation or expanding influence?

"The atomic bomb made the prospect of future war **unendurable**. It has led us up those last few steps to the mountain pass; and beyond there is a different country."
J. Robert Oppenheimer, 1946 ◄

"The use of the atomic bomb, with its indiscriminate killing of women and children, revolts my soul."
► *Herbert Hoover (left), 1945*

World War II came to an end after the U.S. military dropped atomic bombs on the Japanese cities of Hiroshima and Nagasaki in August 1945. The destruction convinced Japan to surrender. Hoover, a former U.S. President who remained active in national politics, was among those who believed nuclear weapons should never have been used. Oppenheimer, the physicist who guided the atomic bomb project, thought that the bomb would save lives by shortening the war—and that no country would dare use it again.

Did the U.S. military make the correct decision in using the atomic bomb during World War II?

"The oil revenues of that country could bring between $50 and $100 billion." *Paul Wolfowitz, 2003* ◀

"I am afraid that Iraq is going to turn out to be the greatest disaster in American **foreign policy**." ▶ *Madeleine Albright, 2006*

Wolfowitz was the Deputy Defense Secretary when the Iraq War began in 2003. The government counted on funds from the oil business to help rebuild the country. Those revenues fell short of expectations. Albright was the first woman in U.S. history to become Secretary of State. She believed that the Iraq War would cause problems for America and its economy.

Should the military weigh the costs in dollars before getting involved in a war?

There has never been a better time to make your voice heard. No matter which side of an issue you take, remember that a debate doesn't have to be an argument. If you enjoy proving your point, join your school's debate team. If your school doesn't have one, find a teacher who will serve as coach and get more students involved. If you want to make a real splash, email the people who represent you in government. If they don't listen now, they may hear from you later … in the voting booth!

GLOSSARY

Abolitionist Movement — An effort in the early 1800s to end slavery in the United States.

Amendment — An addition to the U.S. Constitution.

Atrocities — Cruel and violent acts.

Capitalism — A system of commerce and government that encourages growth through individual profit.

Communism — A system of commerce and government that outlaws private ownership and encourages people to share equally in work and reward.

Cruise Missile — A low-flying weapon that uses a computer to find its target.

Expansionists — A group of politicians in the early 1800s that wanted the U.S. to control as much North American territory as possible.

Foreign Policy — A set of strategies for dealing with other countries, chosen to safeguard national interests.

French and Indian War — A conflict fought in North America from 1754–1763. England and its colonists opposed the French and their Native American allies.

Great Depression — A period of economic upheaval in the U.S. starting in 1929 and ending with World War II.

Infrastructure — The basic organizational and physical elements needed to keep a society up and running, such as roads and sewage systems.

Interrogation — The questioning of people who have been arrested or captured.

Isolationist — Believing in a philosophy that says the U.S. should stay out of overseas conflicts.

Manifest Destiny — A belief that U.S. expansion across the continent was justified and inevitable.

Militias — Groups of citizens who take up arms in an emergency to help a country's regular military.

Muslim — Followers of the Islamic religion.

Neutrality Acts — Laws passed to prevent the U.S. from taking sides in wars between other countries.

Propaganda — Information circulated as part of a political strategy.

Religious Extremists — People willing to go to extraordinary lengths— including violent acts—to further their religious beliefs.

Stalemate — A term from chess meaning a standoff or draw.

Taliban — A religious group that believes in a very strict form of Islam.

Unendurable — Not able to be tolerated.

Vindicate — Clear someone of blame or suspicion.

War of 1812 — A conflict fought between England and the United States from 1812–1814.

Waterboarding — A form of torture meant to make prisoners believe they are drowning.

SOURCES

The authors relied on many different sources for their information. Listed below are some of their primary sources:

For the Common Defense: A Military History of the United States. Allan Reed Millett & Peter Maslowksi. Free Press, New York, 1984.

The Dominion of War: Empire and Liberty in North America 1500–2000. Fred Anderson & Andrew R.L. Clayton. Viking, New York, 2005.

Manifest Destiny: American Expansion and the Empire of Right. Anders Stephanson. Hill & Wang, New York, 1995.

The American West: An Interpretive History. Robert V. Hine. Little, Brown & Co., Boston, 1984.

RESOURCES

For more information on the subjects covered in this book, consider starting with these books and websites:

The Oxford Encyclopedia of American Military and Diplomatic History. Christopher Nichols & David Milne. Timothy J. Lynch & Paul S. Boyer, Editors 2005, New York, New York.

U.S. Army Center of Military History
www.history.army.mil
Good information for historians and great photos of our military.

JuniorGeneral.Org
www.juniorgeneral.org
Refight famous battles through history using printable game pieces. Also, this site has good links to other military history web pages.

INDEX

Page numbers in **bold** refer to illustrations.

AUTHORS

GEOFFREY C. HARRISON and **THOMAS F. SCOTT** are educators at the Rumson
Country Day School, a K thru 8 school in Rumson, New Jersey. Mr. Harrison is the head
of the math department and coordinator of the school's forensics team. Mr. Scott has
been teaching upper school history at RCDS for more than 25 years and is head of that
department. They enjoy nothing more than a great debate … just ask their students!